There's A Jewel In You
Volume 2

THE POWER OF RESILIENCY

Published by
Greater Working Women Publishing, LLC
www.gwwpublishing.com

Providing Publishing Services for Christian Authors & Organizations:
Hardbacks, Paperbacks, E-Books & Audiobooks.

There's A Jewel In You, Volume 2

Copyright © 2018 I Am Still Somebody™

All rights reserved. This book is protected by copyright laws of the United States of America. This book may not be copied or reprinted for commercial gain or profit. The use of short quotations or occasional page copying for personal or group study is permitted and encouraged. Permission will be granted upon request.

Email requests to info@gwwpublishing.com

Ordering Information:
Quantity sales. Special discounts are available on quantity purchases by corporations, associations, and others. For details, contact the publisher at the email address above.

Orders by trade bookstores and wholesalers. Please contact publisher at email address above.

Editor:
LPW Editing & Consulting Services, LLC
www.litapward.com

ISBN: 978-1-948829-04-5

First Edition: April 2018

10 9 8 7 6 5 4 3 2 1

DEDICATION

This book is dedicated to every young mother who is feeling overwhelmed by their situation. You're already RESILIENT! It just hasn't manifested yet! GIVING UP IS NEVER AN OPTION!

I Am Still Somebody™

This is our teen mom mentoring program where we are *Encouraging, Empowering & Equipping Teen Moms To Be Greater Mothers and Greater Women*. Our ministry leader knows first-hand what it feels like to be a teen mom, with all the negativity that is typically associated with it. Our goal as a ministry is to provide teen moms with the knowledge and tools to beat the odds against them.

Our program, which can also be done virtually, is to get teen moms focused and directed on the right track. We will provide free webinars on various topics to help teen moms heal emotionally and address those difficult issues in their life. We also offer valuable life skills they need to achieve greater accomplishments.

We also provide workshops and sessions for organizations that work with teen moms or have a desire to do so. If your organization is interested in hosting a workshop, webinar or ordering any of our resources, please email us at **info@iamstillsomebody.com**.

The next time you see a teen mom please remind them that they are STILL SOMEBODY!

Table of Contents

Introduction — 7

Resilient Hope Conquers Lies — 9

Pregnant: Your Life is Over, But God — 21

Unfinished Does Not Equal Unworthy — 33

Rapes Conception: The Unexpected Way I Entered Motherhood — 45

Life's Contractions — 57

The Power of Daddy Pains — 69

T·E·E·N· MOM — 79

I Am Still Somebody™ — 89

Meet the Authors — 89

INTRODUCTION

They may have counted you out because of your circumstances but it doesn't have to be your reality. You can choose to be a woman of resilience. You can overcome and prove the doubters wrong by going from a statistic to a SUCCESS! Your life is not over because you're a young mother. You're not a failure. You are Still Somebody! You have the power to change the trajectory of your life by the choices you make today. What will you do with your power?

There's A Jewel In You anthology series is written to encourage, empower and equip teen mothers for greater. It takes a JEWEL to see a JEWEL and that's what we see in you! As you read the stories of triumph, picture yourself on the other side of your situation. You're not what they say about you. They never will have that kind of power over you unless you give it to them.

You're already RESILIENT! Now it's time to live like it. What will others read in your life story? There's a Jewel in You!

I Am Still Somebody™

RESILIENT HOPE CONQUERS LIES

One day late, two days late···· Oh God, thirty days had passed since my last menstrual cycle! The thought of this being related to being pregnant caused a fear that I had never felt before in my life. The thoughts that followed threw me into a complete panic. I remembered my mother's words, "If any of you get pregnant, I am throwing you out!" Then I heard, "You're only nine-teen years old; you do not know a thing about being a mother!" and "You've already dropped out of high school; your life is over!" I literally got sick to my stomach as the words continued to beat me down before I had even taken the pregnancy test.

I pleaded with God. "Lord, please don't let me be pregnant." A few days later I told my friend what I was experiencing and mustered up the courage to buy a pregnancy test. My emotions were completely out of control. I thought someone I knew would come in and notice me with the test in my hand. I went back home and took the test as quickly and discreet as I could. I followed the instructions and waited. I peeked over to see the results and saw a positive test result.

I immediately went into denial! So, I went back to get another test. The second test yielded the same results and I lost it right in that bathroom! I wept quietly. "My life is over! She's going to throw me out! People will laugh at me! I am so scared." When I told my boyfriend, he helped me hide the pregnancy from my mother by giving me a robe to cover myself when I was in the house. I wore larger clothes which should have been a dead giveaway, but I hid my pregnancy for almost six months.

Can you imagine the torture? It's only a matter of time that pregnancy can be hidden. I remember standing by the kitchen sink washing the dishes with the robe on. All of a sudden my mother said, "Why do you wear that robe around here all the time?" My heart was racing so fast! She reached to open the robe and her response broke my heart into pieces.

I will say that the words I heard come from her mouth assured me of her pain and disappointment. The months to follow were so hard. It took my mother months to accept that her daughter had followed in her own footsteps. Rejection is not something you want to experience while facing a difficult situation; it makes things so much worse.

Of all the things that I faced as a teen mom, my GREATEST challenge was to get over how I felt about myself. "Failure" was the word I wrote across my heart, and it was reinforced by others. What is the difference between having a baby as a teen and when you're a full grown woman? It is timing, maturity and preparation. The timing was off; I was not mature enough to handle the responsibility, and was certainly not prepared to become a mom.

There were so many things yet to be accomplished, but now my life was over because I was carrying life in me? Lies! I will always be a high school drop out? Lies! I will struggle all my life? Lies! I will never be successful? Lies! Yet, all the lies I believed were destroying me.

I came to the realization that the naysayers and statistics were not my greatest enemy; my greatest enemy was ME. If I could get over ME, I could get over the naysayers and the statistics. First, I had to start with forgiving myself. If we can forgive others, why can't we forgive ourselves? We cannot expect to go through life without ever making wrong decisions. I believe the key is to accept that we did make them and move forward. After all, wherever we have fallen short becomes wisdom to others.

We learn too that we don't see repeated cycles in our lives. I had set goals for my life that would now become delayed, but not denied. Second, I had to embrace the pregnancy, and stop believing that my child was a MISTAKE. A mistake is a misguided action, NOT a child. Third, I had to accept all the responsibility that being mom would bring, including denying myself of the things I had the freedom to do without a child. Fourth, I had to deny all the negative words that would come as the WORD got out.

You see, the negative things can either make you or break you. When I replayed the negative, I would sink so low, but when I would press past the negative, I could see clearly. Why is it so easy for us to believe lies instead of focusing on the truth? I think that has a lot to do with what we think of ourselves. If we haven't entertained the negative, it will not become a part of whom we are.

Finally, I had to know the truth. God STILL loved me and did not see me as a disappointment. His love is unconditional. We don't always choose His best, but His love towards us is unchanging. The truth is He knew about my pregnancy before I did. Life comes from Him no matter what age factor. There is a time for everything, and getting ahead of that timing can bring experiences that were designed for us to handle later on in life.

The doctor's visits, the stares, and the anxiety of giving birth were so paralyzing, but I still had to embrace the process. I had to deny my favorite foods, stop clubbing, and deny all the other things I had freedom to do before I became pregnant. Life was no longer about Yerinita; life became about the child who was growing inside of me. I can tell you this was not what I had planned, but it was the result of not being responsible.

It was so important for me to surround myself with people that would say, "You can make it." Please know that there will always be a crowd to help you fail. However, there will also be a few that will help you in positive ways. God sent me people that encouraged me to keep going. They helped me to see motherhood from a different perspective and to see myself in a different light.

God is a loving Father and will never leave us to fend for ourselves no matter the circumstances. The truth is life is not over until it's really over. We can conquer the lies or accept them. Both responses shape our mentality. God created me and my baby girl with purpose, and being a mom at an early age does not CANCEL His plans. I know God wanted me to wait until I was ready, but that doesn't mean it took Him by surprise.

So, I was a mom now. What were the additional things I had to do? Delete the word "FAILURE" from my life. Failure is not a person, it's an event; REPLACE the word "failure" with SUCCESS. It would be more challenging with a child but I could still SUCCEED. God granted me the tenacity to see past everything that I had done wrong, and helped me focus on what could be made right. This was the beginning of me defying all the odds.

Perseverance, endurance, and tenacity was the character that I had to personally develop. There were many obstacles I had to overcome; however, I was determined to prove to myself and others that my story would be different. I was able to withstand because my mind changed from victim to victor. I can say that I had to learn how to be a mom, hands-on. I tapped into a love for her that was almost destroyed with my negative thinking even while she was in my womb. The voice of hope spoke to me every day and said, "Yerinita, do it for her. Give her a chance. Give her what you were missing. You can do this." It was hard and exhausting but I decided to give her my all. Some days I thought I would just lose my mind, but I held on to hope. Hope is an expectation of change. Hope will keep you, if you want to be kept.

So how did things turn out you might ask? Well, I'm no longer a high school dropout. I obtained my G.E.D and years later signed up for college and obtained my first degree. I worked and went to school and God provided others to help me accomplish my goals. My baby was deeply loved by me and that love has shaped her life even right now. I am married now with seven beautiful children. And yes, he is the father of all my children. It's only by the grace of God we walked away from our rebellious lifestyles and turned to God. I know that our story is rare but it's definitely possible.

I dedicate my life to helping others avoid or overcome things I went through in my youth and adult years. This is how we put purpose to our pain. There are so many who need hope and we are sharing our stories with you for that reason. It's not over until it's over. It's not over until God is done, and if He is not done, He is not finished.

I live to empower women both young and old to persevere through life's obstacles. There is light at the end of the tunnel, God's guiding light. Who will you allow to dictate your outcome as a teen mom? It all comes down to a choice. You determine your outcome by what you believe about yourself. You do not have to succumb to failure and be a statistic. You can choose to lose or win.

    Will you persevere and be all God created you to be or allow all that purpose to go to waste? Have you convinced yourself that you cannot succeed as a teen mom? I have learned that what we feed the most will win. Perhaps you can do what I and so many other have done. We have turned that statistic around and proved it wrong. The key is to focus on the goal, not the process. If you focus on the process the goals may seem impossible. The most beautiful things happen in the middle. So, you're a teen mom? What's next? Whatever you decide, do not let it be to QUIT. As long as you have life you can be successful. It's your choice; what will it be?

~Yerinita Curtis-Fuller

Failure is not a person, it's an event; REPLACE the word "failure" with SUCCESS.

PREGNANT: YOU'RE LIFE IS OVER, BUT GOD!

As a child, I struggled with depression and anxiety early on as a result of sexual trauma that I experienced by someone close to me. I did not disclose this until adulthood and because of that, I suffered silently for a long time. I was never treated professionally during my adolescence for my mental health or trauma related issues and had a difficult time accepting myself as being worthy of God's best.

Early on, I had a relationship with Christ, attending Sunday school with my grandmother most weekends. I also went to a Christian elementary school and was taught that we should abstain, however, due to the sexual trauma that I endured, I never felt like a virgin. Yet, I did want to save what I felt was left of myself for my future husband. I grew up being taught by my parents that I could be whatever I wanted to be and college was a major part of their vision for my success. When people would ask me what I wanted to do when I got older, I would reply with the same list of jobs: "Actress, Singer, Dancer, Social Worker, Writer, and Teacher." Overtime, I'd narrow my list down though.

    I made it all the way until my senior year of high school with a clear vision of who I wanted to be and what I wanted to do. I had big dreams of leaving for college and starting my life of journalism at one of the best performing arts schools, Columbia College in Chicago. Along the way, I began dating someone who was very different from others I had encountered. He often shared with me that he had a rough upbringing and just wanted a chance to do better. I was intrigued by him because he was so different and I honestly felt like I could help him to get on the straight and narrow path. It wasn't long into our relationship before we became intimate. It was only a few months to be frank. I decided he was the one even if God hadn't said so and anyone who disagreed with me, pushed me more to prove them wrong.

During our relationship, he and I spent more time apart than together due to him being incarcerated. He got out in July and by August, I was pregnant. I had already applied and been accepted to my college of choice when I suspected that I was pregnant at age eighteen. School started in September, so I felt like I had time to make a decision about what I was going to do with our baby.

Fearful yet determined, I still went to school and stayed in the dormitory for a semester.

Staying on campus and going to college while pregnant was very hard for me. The entire time I was in a state of denial of my pregnancy which made me consider alternative options. Yes, I considered not keeping my child and as painful as that is to admit, it's the truth. I contemplated the idea of adoption; however, some members of my family had other plans and wanted me to abort. I just couldn't do it. Though I knew sex was a sin, I recognized the baby as being a blessing even if that meant it wasn't mine to keep.

I remember riding the train to class when I saw an ad overhead that read, "Pregnant & Confused? Call us." I searched in my bag, digging around for a pen and paper. I knew this was the answer to my prayers in what route to go. I took the number down and exited the train. During class, I couldn't focus. My body was physically there, but my mind wasn't. I hadn't actually taken a pregnancy test at that point although it had been months without my menstrual cycle. I was living in denial, thinking if I didn't hear it, then it wasn't true. I believed that they could help me though, so as soon as I could, I called them. I got the name and location, then made an appointment to go see them. Now I just had to find a way to get there. I called my dad because I knew he'd help me. We were always close and there was little he'd say no to. I just wasn't ready to tell him exactly where I was going and why. Thankfully, he didn't really ask many questions when I asked him to take me.

That day we rode to the pregnancy center in silence. It resembled a small home in the suburbs, so I figured it wouldn't be too much of a giveaway. That's when I saw the sign *PASS*. I hoped my dad wouldn't figure out that it was an acronym nor what it stood for. I needed to know how these people could help me. I wasn't prepared for what happened next. I went *inside alone while my dad waited in the car and told the receptionist my name. I waited in the lobby just a short time before an older woman called me to the back. She took me into a room to ask me questions about my pregnancy. Of course, she wanted to know how far along I was, but I didn't know. She gave me a pregnancy test; I took it and we waited. It didn't take long for the lines to pop up as positive for pregnancy.*

My heart raced as I hoped what I saw was wrong. I could no longer live in denial. I was pregnant. She took my hand and asked if she could share something with me. I said yes and she proceeded to tell me a story of her sister who had aborted her baby and explained that for years after, she still couldn't get over the fact that she had an abortion. She didn't want me to live with that regret and neither did I. However, I didn't think being a mom was an option for me, only adoption. She listened to me then asked if she could pray with me. It was then that I knew I couldn't give my child away. The way she prayed for me and the story she shared are forever ingrained in my memory. The staff took it a step further and gave me a year supply of all the baby's basic needs for free, including a crib! Now, I just needed to figure out how I could break the news to my family, starting with my dad who was in the car this whole time!

Once I got back in the car, I asked my father if he knew where we were and he responded, "Yes." It was then that I confirmed my pregnancy. He didn't seem happy or upset. In fact, he didn't have much of a reaction, but we knew that I had to tell my mom. Although I was 18 and technically out of the house, I still depended on them for many things. Telling my mom was much more difficult and her reaction was less than favorable. It was then that I was told my life was over; but God!

I was determined to prove that statement to be false. I didn't know what or how, but I knew that I had to do something. As a result of my pregnancy, my family didn't pay my college tuition and I was left with no other option than to drop out. One semester of college wasted and I couldn't use the credits. Before having to leave the dorm, I was called on the phone and told to get ready that my dad was picking me up to have an abortion. I have never been more afraid in my life. I didn't want to be a mom, but I didn't want to have an abortion either so I ran away. Before he could get there, I called my boyfriend and we met up. I hid out at his house until I was sure that the office hours had passed. I even asked his family to cover for me if my family called looking for me and they did.

Later on, I remember talking to my sister who gave me information for prenatal care because I still hadn't had any form of treatment and by then I was approaching five months. She gave me the best advice that I still carry with me until today. "This is your baby. Don't rely on anyone to help you, not even the father." I used the advice as motivation to be as self-sufficient as possible with my daughter in tow. Of course, we all need help, but I was determined not to live under the cursed words that my life was over.

Throughout the course of my pregnancy, I was physically abused by my partner. It was a rough time for me because I didn't truly feel like I had the support of anyone. I did have a childhood friend, however, who talked to me about the possibility of relocating to DeKalb, Illinois, for school and the many resources they had for single mothers. I thought about her suggestion and started searching for affordable housing near the community college out there. I went to visit and made up in my mind then that my child and I would start anew once I had her. My decision came with some resistance thought. My family was a little more accepting of my pregnancy by now, but shared their concerns about me being so far and alone with a newborn. They also worried that I may not be safe from my then partner as the abuse had escalated. I had some concerns, but I was excited about the opportunity to try. I took my chances and my daughter and I thrived. I was not only able to get my college degree, but it was there that in my solitude, I was able to restore my relationship with Christ.

I won't pretend it was easy; it was far from it, but one thing I know to be true is that anything is possible with God. Since that time, my daughter and I have overcome many obstacles together. God gave me wisdom to raise her with Him as our foundation and blessed us to be more than any limiting statistics on what happens to the offspring of teenage parents. I was told that my life was over when I revealed my pregnancy, but God! He has blessed and kept us through it all. To the teen mom reading this: Your life is not over. You still have purpose and those dreams you once had can still be accomplished. Use your situation to learn and grow. You have someone depending on you to make it.

~Whit Devereaux

"This is your baby. Don't rely on anyone to help you, not even the father."

Unfinished does not Equal Unworthy

"Everybody get on the floor!" That's what the officer yelled as the police raided the place I called home. My twin brother and I were somewhere between three and five years of age when Bridgeport police kicked in the door of the crack house we lived in with our mother and grandmother. I remember sitting there, aware. Not scared, not sad, just aware. Aware of what had become normal for me. This wasn't the first time the crack house had been raided and it certainly wouldn't be the last, but this time it was different.

As they dragged several people away in handcuffs, I realized my mother was one of them. She was high and seemingly clueless as to what was going on. As my grandmother held us, high herself, the last officer looked at her and said, "Next time we'll be taking them with us," as he pointed to my brother and I. And then, they were gone. Just as fast as they invaded our "home," they were gone.

Not too long thereafter, maybe a few days or so, we received yet another surprise visit. Late in the night, I heard a knock on the door and when my grandmother opened it, in they came like soldiers. One grabbed me and the other scooped up my brother. Just like that, we were now in the custody of the Department of Children and Families and life as we knew it would never be the same. I eventually was adopted by the Mayfield family when I was 8 years old.

My adopted parents did the best they could to raise me and by no means did I live a bad life. I lived in a nice, clean home. I was always dressed nice, went to private schools, had home cooked meals every night, and even took summer vacations. My mother and father took very good care of me; I never lacked for what I needed. But even with all of those things that I was provided, there were things that I desired that were more important to me than the things that I needed.

Webster's Dictionary says that to nurture is to "feed or nourish." A mother's nurture is fuel for the soul. Good mothers pour care into the souls of their children much like sunlight and water pour nutrients into a plant. Our souls flourish when we are being nurtured and cared for. We grow, develop, and change according to the way we were designed. And that is exactly what I desired; to be nurtured.

You must remember that I was taken from my birth mother at a very young age. While pregnant with my brother and I, our mother was addicted to drugs. After we were born, my mother continued to spend the majority of her time on the streets instead of nurturing her young. After we were removed from our home and our mother, we were placed in a foster home where unfortunately we were only two of many.

Nurturing was almost nonexistent there as well. By the time we arrived to our adopted parents, I was dying to be nurtured. I was in need of someone that was going to encourage me, support me, motivate me, push me, tell me they loved me, hug me, wipe my tears, etc. Needless to say, that's not what my mom had to offer. She provided me with what I needed, not what I desired. By the time I was 15, my desire to be nurtured could almost be compared to an addiction. It was all I could think about.

So during the summer, leading into my sophomore year of high school, I decided to search for my birth family. That summer was amazing. I was able to locate some of my birth mother's family and get to look into the eyes of people that I looked alike. I was able to hear stories about my birth mother and learn that we shared a lot of some of the same traits. Unfortunately, she was back in prison, so the nurturing that I desired from my mother was still not an option.

Amongst other things, for the first time I was introduced to young men, dating and sex for the first time. At the age of 18, I met a young man who I just knew I would marry. He seemed like the perfect guy. He was a sweetheart, had a job, and his own car. We had been dating for only a few months before we began having sex and I moved into his father's home with him. He already had two children at the time from a previous relationship, which I later learned, had just ended weeks before we met.

Although I cannot say that he was a bad father, I knew he wasn't the best father. Furthermore, I knew he wasn't ready to be a father to another child, but that didn't stop me from desiring to have a baby with him. If I'm honest with myself, that desire stemmed from a place of jealously; jealous that his ex-girlfriend had a connection with him that would always be bigger than mine.

So although I didn't purposely try to get pregnant, I did nothing not to either. From that mismanaged decision we created a life that we weren't mature enough to comprehend the level of responsibility that it would take to be successful. I didn't call my adopted family right away and share the news of my pregnancy because a big part of me was ashamed. I wasn't raised to have a child out of wedlock or even to be living with a man while not married, but here I was, living a life the exact opposite of how I was raised. So I did it alone. My pregnancy was quite intense. Not only was it high risk due to me developing a pregnancy disease called cholestasis, which caused my skin to severely itch within my blood stream, but I also found out my perfect man, had impregnated another young woman just before meeting me. Yup, that would be the reason he and his ex-girlfriend ended things! And she had just given birth to their child.

Due to my cholestasis, I had to have an emergency C-section two months before my due date. My son was a preemie, weighing in at just 4lbs at birth. He was the smallest person I had ever held, but he rocked my world in a major way. He gave me that same feeling I felt when I was first taken from my birth mom; I felt aware. Now aware that my life would never be the same because I had a life that depended on me.

One day, my son's grandfather had me to come downstairs to his apartment. He sat me in a chair and handed me a mirror. He said, "Look into this mirror and tell me who you see." It was the first time in a very long time that I looked in a mirror and didn't recognize the face staring back at me. Somewhere along the way, I had fought so hard for someone to love me that I stopped fighting to love myself. It was at that moment that I woke up from out of the nightmare I had been living in. I immediately jumped into gear.

I moved into my first apartment in the projects, enrolled in a medical coding program, enrolled my son into a childcare program and got a part-time job. One thing I had learned from being in foster care was how to survive. My son's father and I remained together for two years. Those two years would have to have been the worst years of my life. There were times when as a mother, my only job was to cuddle and love this new life that God had gifted me with, but instead I chased after and fought for someone to love me, who wasn't qualified. I put the life that God entrusted me with in compromising situations.

I allowed him to see me cry and fight. I allowed him to see me weak with no control of my choices and yet he loved me. As God increased the years of his life, he witnessed me learning to love myself so I could love him better. What I didn't see was the damage I had caused. I didn't see the pain he was hiding. While I thought I was making the best decisions for his, life it would be those same decisions that would later cause him to struggle to love himself.

Although I've done the best I could do, provided him with all his material needs, I deprived him of his spiritual needs which would have undergirded his mental needs. My son will be 16 in just a few short months. I look at him and I can't believe that we have overcome so much...together. When my son was 2 ½ years old, I met and later married a God-sent man. Together we have worked hard to mold and shape our son into a really good young man. He's kind, loving, funny, and smart. I look into his eyes and I see so many dreams that I have for him. I see him as a dedicated husband, a loving father, and a hardworking man. I now thank God that I can be what I spent most of my life searching for, a nurturing mother.

To my fellow teen mothers, as you walk on this new path in your life, remember that you are still growing, you are still learning and evolving into the women that God has created you to be. You are unfinished, but you are not unworthy. When the voices of the doubters are screaming in your ears, allow God's truth to drown out the noise.

When you listen to the Truth, which is God's Word, not your own thoughts or the opinions of others, you will hear Him say things like, "Oh (Insert your name here), you don't always get it right, but I still love you. Look through my eyes and see what I see; my beautiful creation, my treasure, my masterpiece. The sooner you see yourself for who you really are, the sooner you can take your reign as my priceless princess with a purpose - My masterpiece. You were created in my image and you are indeed a piece of the Master." Can you hear Him? It doesn't matter what you've done or even what you're doing at this very second, God's love never fails. He is waiting for you to look through His eyes and see yourself as He created you....a MASTERPIECE!

"For we are God's masterpiece. He has created us anew in Christ Jesus, so we can do the good things he planned for us long ago."
Ephesians 2:10 (NLT)

Rape's Conception:
The Unexpected Way I Entered Motherhood

A woman of color, a woman of ability, a woman with desires, a woman with a dream. A woman who has constantly overlooked myself and how much I am worth. I am living in a sense where my life is only a movie, but a movie that would end in failure. I work hard and I am stronger than ever but can't seem to see success in this "movie" I entitled, "I don't know." Why are you upset? What is your purpose? Why are you doing what you are doing? How are you? The answer has always been, "I don't know." I even looked down on myself in settings I knew I shined brightly.

It was the summer of my sixth grade year when I experienced pain because God was getting ready to birth something in my life. It all happened when I was twelve years old. One push to the ground, one stomp to the head, one hit to my back, a drag to this house and a big loss of my womanhood. "Unzip your pants, take off that shirt, lay back and you bet' not scream. Oh and I wish you would move!" I started to scream and I got one hit to my face. Now I'm lying there and I can't do anything. I cried in silence for about 30 long minutes. I just knew my life was over. I couldn't believe that was happening to me. I suffered from a lot of bruises, blood loss, and pain that felt like I was being attacked by a tiger. After he finished, he said, "If you tell anyone what happened to you, I'll kill you." That's exactly what I did; I didn't tell anyone. No one noticed I was gone for so long and no one questioned my scars, so I hid my pains and truth.

My family didn't know, so I started my seventh grade year hoping that something would change since I was entering a new school and a new environment. Then, the months went by. After the first five months, I started feeling mood changes. Two more months went by and now I got this feeling that I may be pregnant, but I couldn't believe that was true. No one knew for sure, but I knew everyone did start to wonder as well. It was like a dream but instead it was reality. I woke up Friday morning, April 15, 2011 getting ready for school, but I had this pain that came every five minutes or so. The day and moment that I didn't want to come had arrived. It was the day I found out I was pregnant after being raped and it was the day the world found out I was pregnant. They didn't know my story because I disguised it. I was in labor and didn't even know what I was having. I was in labor for only two hours and I can remember the doctors saying, "It's a boy. No, It's a girl," as they were fooled by the amount of hair she had. I mean that moment was priceless I must say. I just couldn't believe it was happening.

I was pounded with questions and all my answers were, "I don't know." I was afraid of all the misconceptions and assumptions. It was me against the world and at that point, I had to ask myself, "Would they judge me? Would they see me as others?" So there I was thirteen with a daughter. I thought I wasn't going to have the help or support, so I decided I wanted to give her up for adoption, I didn't even want to see her. As I was lying in the hospital bed I was in denial of what happened and immediately thought that my daughter would be better off with someone who was ready. I was still a child myself and I assumed that my abilities would not be good enough to take care of a child. I just knew I was sure about that, but I remembered holding her before I left the hospital and the smile on my face and joy in my heart. Two days later I said, "No, I want my child." She was still a part of me. She didn't ask to be here and there was no handbook on how to be a mother, so I figured I had the title and it was time for me to hold it. It was tough because I got judged and talked about for a long time. I mean I was the talk of the neighborhood and talk of the school. It was unbelievable! I felt like I had missed out on everything and most of all a teenage dream. I had a daughter and I was only thirteen. I felt like I jumped into reality and it had just begun.

 While I was bearing new life, I felt as if mine was ending. It was hard to envision a future worth striving towards. It affected me in school because I was known as the "smart Alexis" but then it transformed as the "Alexis with the baby." I was hurt by the truth and I found more comfort in sharing my hopes, fears, and life with a pen and paper. It was my way of bringing those words and thoughts on the paper to life. This heightened my desire to learn more about how to write. Writing was like my only way out of not talking and a way of expressing my real, true feelings. I grew up really quickly and everything happened fast, but I took on a challenge that I knew would be hard to face. I was determined that I could be the best mother a child could ask for at a young age. At first, it was heartbreaking, but I could not let my past determine my future. It took one Saturday night of pain and suffering and one Friday morning of pain and joy to embark me into a journey worth going after. It was my time to tell everyone the true story behind me being "Alexis with the baby."

    I realized that from the depths of my challenges could emerge peaks of inspiration. The experiences that I once held hostage could now liberate me from my distrust of the world. I pledged to speak and shift my truths, pains, and life experiences into a message of triumph and hope that others could relate to, learn from and feel empowered by. Once I began to believe in the good of others, I was able to emerge into the best version of myself. After that realization, I decided that I could no longer be deterred by my challenges, but that I had to persist and break down the walls I had built to once protect me from the cruelties of life. I turned into my true self, by not allowing others to bring me down, which was honestly just a smart girl who strived for good grades. I realized that I was not the only person who had gone through the situations I had, so there was no excuse to end my success. The thought of everything I had to go through at such a young age makes me very sad and disappointed, but even more so honored and dedicated because I am who I am and I am going to continue to work my hardest. I've been through a lot but it is not close to being over. If you want something to get done and to start a movement for change or for the better, there is a voice. We all have a voice now, but my voice will be heard.

The day I became a mother, it opened my eyes. I then knew that it was up to me to raise a bright, intelligent, young woman. Motherhood has taught me to think ahead of my future. I was the outsider in class who everyone would talk about and think less of by what they assumed the case may have been. I had to deal with a lot of assumptions people made. Also, as a student I learned discipline so I was able to understand the concept behind the teachers' actions or words.

There have been times where my life meant nothing to me. I used to continuously have flashbacks. I chose to not wear makeup, getting my nails done, and stopped getting my hair done. I even started to dress like a tomboy. Anything that had to do with me being pretty or an attraction to someone was the route I didn't want to go. I had let someone destroy my womanhood. Once I opened up, talking about my story was like talking about a trip to the beach. I never have a hard time letting it out and I am able to say everything with confidence. My daughter really has given me a different outlook on life in general and has taught me discipline. I didn't know that my mom had taken on a lot of responsibilities when she had kids and I didn't know why mothers were so overprotective. I was just not fully understanding that language.

I knew that I had to take on motherly "duties" as we call it. A lot had changed instantly and I knew that if I still wanted to be a kid, I had to find out how to be a mother first. It is a lot to learn when you become a parent and with the help of my mother, I am the best mom that I can be to my daughter. My pregnancy and my mom helped me to be not only a mother, but a young mature adult that can prove to everyone age is nothing but a number and that I can raise a child just like anyone else. What will help you?

I want you to use this in the future to teach someone that no matter what the circumstances may be, be true to who you are. Don't do anything you will regret, and always remember you are never in it alone. I want you to be the one to tell someone that it is okay to cry, it is okay not to be okay and most importantly you can overcome anything obstacle that life throws at you. I am a living witness of overcoming a huge obstacle to find my path. I am no longer living in a world of "I don't know" and my life has been a success. Never doubt your abilities of being a woman and never let someone attack your anointing! I am here to tell you that there is power in your pain.

~Alexis

Don't do anything you will regret, and always remember you are never in it alone.

Life's Contractions

I was the eldest of three children, second to go to college in my immediate family, currently on academic probation from school, losing my fight with depression and feeling completely alone due to the strained relationship between my mother and me. I wasn't a rebellious child but I was very head strong and independent just as my mom and grandma raised me to be. But my mom wanted to control every aspect of my life, just as I had often seen my grandma attempt to do with her. I just wanted to find my own way and because of that, I ended up on my own for a while once I graduated high school entering college. My mom and grandma had taught me to be the best that I could be, yet the harder I tried to show them, the tighter it seemed my mom held on which resulted in me pulling farther away. College introduced me to many things, good and bad, but I never lost sight of my upbringing or morals and I acted as such. No, I wasn't a perfect angel; I lived life's screw ups and all. While facing many of college life's ups and downs, the broken relationship between my mom and I left me feeling as though I was alone. As a result, I began slipping into a depression and no one even noticed.

I met my future baby-daddy, Aaron, around the age of 19 at a homecoming event. Upon our meeting, Aaron informed me he was 24; okay a five years age difference. That's no big deal, right? I later found out that he was nine years my elder while cleaning out his pockets as I was doing our laundry, but I was already knocked up by then and we were living together. There was never anything serious between Aaron and me beyond random contact by phone over the next year. The first two years of college were filled with fun, adventures, parties, laughter and learning.

But as I entered my third year, life seemed to have it in for me and there were no breaks in between the blows. I ended up on academic probation, and I didn't have a place to stay because I lived in the dorms. I was staying in my friend's Zena's dorm room while I was trying to get things figured out. Christmas break was approaching so Zena invited me to spend the holidays with her and her family. Zena's family welcomed me with open arms and once they learned of my situation, offered that I stay with them while I worked in order to get my own place and get on my feet. Thank you God for answering my prayers or so I thought.

One day while I was standing in the bathroom, Zena's father approached me with a proposition to either be pimped out to his son or pose for nude pictures which would be sold in effort him to support his drug habit. The walls seemed to begin caving in on me. Did no one love me? Why me?! Staying there was no longer an option, so I begin trying to figure out who I could call. My list was slim to non-existent and the ones I did call didn't respond.

Finally as a last resort, I called Aaron and told him everything. I didn't want to be a burden to anyone; besides he and I really didn't know each other, but I was desperate. Aaron drove from Louisiana to north Arkansas that same day to get me. I stayed with him for the rest of the holiday break and returned right before school started back. Due to the nature of my relationship with Aaron, I didn't want to impose on him, since we were really still getting to know each other. I now couldn't attend school because I didn't have the money needed to pay for tuition.

Upon my return, my moods began to change uncontrollably and I didn't even notice until one day, I had eaten all of the pickles and wanted Zena to take me to get some more because I didn't have a car at the time. She wouldn't and I was absolutely devastated and angry with her. She told me then I was pregnant. She had noticed my mood changes and my extreme sleeping and eating habits. Not me or so I thought. Still in need of a place to stay I had ran completely out of options and was venting to Aaron about it, when he provided the solution to all my problems. He told me to come live with him until I got on my feet and not to worry about anything else. He again made a trip to Arkansas for me, but this time I wasn't returning.

A couple of weeks after I got settled in, I had to

be taken to the hospital for an extreme case of dehydration. The doctor informed me that I was pregnant. Truth is, I already knew that; I had taken a test about a week prior but I was in denial. That was the last thing I needed in my life right now. The night I was taken to the hospital, Aaron was with someone else.

The next morning when he came home, I told him I was pregnant. I didn't expect him to be overjoyed by this because we weren't in a relationship nor had we ever talked about it. But he was cool with it; then he proceeded to inform me that a young lady he was dealing with was pregnant also. The other young lady later had an abortion but I didn't. I told Aaron that the baby didn't ask to be here and this was a result of our actions. So I kept the baby and he was okay with my decision. We decided to give the relationship a try for the sake of the baby. My family still didn't know I was pregnant but I knew I needed to tell them because I wouldn't be able to hide it much longer.

I took Aaron home to meet my family and it went as good as one would hope according to the situation. My grandpa being very traditional put marriage on the table upfront, but I didn't want that. Aaron asked me about it once we returned home and I told him no. He and I had not talked about marriage and I didn't want to force it. I plan to only marry once to the man God created just for me and deep down I didn't believe that was Aaron.

As I progressed through my pregnancy, things with Aaron and I got worse with each argument. Once again, there was another woman Sadie, but this argument led me to threatening to take Aaron's life and sitting at the front door awaiting his arrival to stab him in the head with the fire poker. It was time to go, but where? One day I received a call from a childhood friend asking if I was okay. I didn't understand her reason for asking so she proceeded to inform me that my mom had told some individuals that she wanted no part of me or my bastard baby's life. Again here I was feeling all alone with no peace and I couldn't even begin to know where to look for it.

Six months into my pregnancy, I was taken to the hospital where the doctor informed me I was having contractions five minutes apart; basically I was in labor. At that time my daughter only weighed eight ounces; to give birth to her right then would be terminal for her and possibly me too. They eventually got my contractions to cease; I was put on bed rest for the rest of my pregnancy. I had to leave my job and several days later, I got a call from my grandma telling me to come home so that they could take care of me.

For the first time after all I had been dealing with, I heard the words "Come home." I packed up all my things one weekend while Aaron was out of town with Sadie and returned home to Arkansas. Two weeks later, I had my daughter Amani Victoria, August 17, 2004 at 11:57am. She was 4 weeks early, but within that two-week time frame, I was able to get my weight up and my baby girl's weight also. We had to stay in the hospital for three days due to her being premature, but she was absolutely beautiful and healthy.

I stayed with my family for a year to make sure that Amani and I were okay. Amani's birth caused my family to focus on something other than ourselves and we slowly began rebuilding our relationship but not without obstacles. I enrolled back in school a year later, but was unable to transfer my credits to the new college; therefore, I had to start over as a freshman. Devastated but determined, I started school and found a job. I had to finish what I started for the sake of Amani; I needed her to understand that anything is possible when you put your mind to it.

Obstacles will come but that's life. But how you handle the obstacles is up to you. Aaron was more of a hindrance than help in the years to follow. The relationship with my mom began to fall apart again as well; she just couldn't relinquish control. I had to understand that God would provide everything and everyone we needed. When that happened, I let Aaron and all pertaining to him go and let God. Five years later with Amani back and forth between me and my family, living in not-so-safe neighborhoods, failing some courses, heartbreaks, mental breakdowns, homelessness, hunger, hopelessness, being stalked by my mom and more, I walked across the stage and received my Bachelor's degree in Business of May 2010.

Growing up, I saw myself finishing college, starting a career, getting married, buying a home, raising a family and helping others as much as I could. That wasn't exactly how it happened for me though, but I know that all the things that have not yet happened are in the works right now. During those five years, my mother and grandmother called me an unfit mother, attempted to take my daughter, and threatened to call Child Protective Services. My mother would even come into town and follow me without my knowledge.

In spite of everything, I am grateful for being taught about God growing up. I prayed that He would heal my heart as well as my mother's heart. My relationship with my mom is still a work in progress daily and I love her just as I always have. I only have one and I thank God for her. She has given and gives her best, both good and bad. After graduation, I moved to Texas for better opportunities. Once I got settled, I brought Amani out with me. Yes, I am a single mother and I still face struggles every day, but I am beyond grateful for my journey with my daughter. God used my daughter to save my life; she's one of my earth angels.

~Christina

The Power of Daddy Pains

My name is Avery and I have three children, under three years old; all before the age of 23. This is my story of how I overcame the hurt of being a young mother. I became a mother at the age of 18 with my first child, my second at 21 and was a mother of three by the age of 22. I was in a serious relationship with a guy who I absolutely thought was the guy of my dreams. My situation was a lot deeper than most because I was pregnant back to back. I allowed this guy into my heart and then I soon later began to be intimate with him and it resulted in getting pregnant. The relationship was very unhealthy, but I wasn't aware of the red flags in the beginning, so I continued to stay. When you're in love with someone, it's sometimes difficult to recognize the signs that you're not being treated as well as you should be. The thought of knowing that I had conceived, and birthed three beautiful children was an amazing, but also a scary feeling! I suffered from deep depression and I was truly ashamed of the poor decisions that I had made to not only protect myself sexually, but to not be aware of the damage that I was doing to myself emotionally and physically. I lost many friends because of my decision to keep my children.

I went from being very popular in high school to becoming the girl that got pregnant over the summer break. I couldn't move forward with my peers to college because while others were preparing their dorms, I was preparing a nursery to become a mother. The decision to keep my children was not hard at all; it was the fear of what others would think of me. My biggest battle that I struggled with most, was not only being a young parent but dealing with the abuse that my children's dad had exhibited. I struggled with not only physical abuse, but also verbal and emotional abuse. Abuse can also be psychological, and I buried the behavior for fear of losing what I thought was a family for myself and my children. The individual whom I thought was the guy of my dreams turned into my worst nightmare; and the more I tried to leave, the worse the abuse got. So I stayed... I stayed because I felt my children deserved both of their parents in one home, no matter how bad he would beat me. I wanted that family picture to make me feel whole. I hid behind scars and bruises because eventually it felt normal in such a way that I grew numb to the pain. Some would ask, "Why would you put up with such despicable, and destructive behavior from an individual who is supposed to love you?" Questions like that were easy to ask because they've never been in a situation so deep like the one I was in. Abusive relationships are like spider webs that trap the victim in a cycle of confusion, fear, hope, and despair. I grew up not knowing my biological father, which left a hole in my heart that I thought having my kids could fill. I desired that family picture so much that I tolerated a lot just to keep that image of a family.

But the more I stayed the more I became depressed and the more I lost myself. I became insecure about my body image, I had no friends to turn and talk to who could really relate to not only being a young mother, but being abused as well. I ultimately felt worthless. So here I was not only raising three children under three alone, but I was dealing with some deep issues as well. I was afraid to ask for help because I was so ashamed, and my pride wouldn't allow me to seek the help that I needed. The abuse was so deep that I even started lying to those who cared about me the most. Until one day, God showed me my value and my worth! He allowed me to see that there was purpose in my pain and victory in my sorrow. I was able to rediscover Avery and all she had to offer, and I was able to deal with the deep-rooted issues that I've had for many years. I was able to finally get the strength that I needed for myself and my children to just leave. I had the help of my parents and close family members to really push me to my purpose, and to be free. Leaving helped me to clear my head and realize that I had "Daddy Pains" which led me to be in an unhealthy relationship; and also poisoned my mind of believing that having children and a family of my own would even fill that void of a broken home.

God broke me to position me and helped me get out of my unhealthy relationship. I've learned through my dark season that staying doesn't provide a better home, having an abuse-free home does. I also learned that just because I became a mother early doesn't mean God doesn't have a purpose and a plan for my life. He showed me that my babies were never a mistake, but merely examples of His grace and mercy that He shows us in spite of our sinful actions. Leaving was hard, but it was doable! The pain was hard to bear at times, but after a while I looked in the mirror and realized... WOW! After all those hurts, scars, people talking down at me, and after all the trials I faced, I really made it through. I DID IT! I literally survived that which was supposed to kill me. I also learned that one of the best feelings is finally losing your attachment to somebody who isn't good for you. I'm so glad that God placed certain individuals in my life to help push me through those dark days and to overcome the abuse and pain that it caused.

If I had a chance to speak to my younger self I would simply tell her... "Hey little girl; the one with the long pretty hair and beautiful skin! Do you know that you're beautiful and smart? Do you know that God has great plans for your life, or do you believe what others say about you never fitting in? Dear younger me, I want you to know that you are great, and you are fearfully and wonderfully made. I wish you had loved yourself a little more than you did, but most importantly, I wish that you would have listened to the voice of God a little more than you did and had sought validation from Him and not man."

My prayer every day is that God would enlarge my territory so that others may be healed. He heals the brokenhearted and binds up their wounds (Psalm

147:3). I hope that for the young girl reading this you will overcome anything that is hurting you or making you feel that having a baby will fill the void of your pain. I pray that any obstacle you face as a young mother you will face it head-on, knowing that God is always with you and that He will never leave you or forsake you. I also hope that any woman reading this, knows that God forgives you for every unplanned pregnancy or bad decision you have made. Know that your baby is not a mistake or an act of the devil because God is the giver of life and His plan is so much greater than our minds and hearts could ever imagine. Being a young mother doesn't mean that your life is over, it just means that you have your own personal cheerleader cheering you along the way to success. My experience as a young mother had not only pushed me to strive for better, but it has made me better. I honestly believe that my life wouldn't have been this amazing if I didn't have my children along side of me pushing me to be the great mother that I am and the wonderful woman of God that I'm becoming. I overcame the hurt of being a young mother by working hard for what I now have and continuing to focus on my goals that I've set for myself. I truly allowed God into my heart; now I am thinking deeper, and loving myself a lot more than I have ever done before. I also didn't allow fear to manifest in my heart or poison the dreams that I have of being a great mother and business owner. My drive and motivation are knowing that my children are happy and that my hustle is never in vain.

~Avery

You are already RESILIENT! You just haven't looked in the mirror yet.

T·E·E·N· MOM

Triumphing· Embracing· Empowering· Never-Failing·

"Don't Degrade Me Because I'm A Teen Mother; Help Me Because I'm Willing To Learn"

I believe every young girl has sat on the floor, playing with her dolls and imagined all the things she wanted to be and accomplish as an adult· I clearly remember all the wonderful visions that danced in my head day after day as a child· I wanted the perfect marriage (thanks Barbie and Ken for that imagery), live in a nice house with a fence, a cute dog running around, have the perfect job and be the mother to two children, a boy and a girl. Of course, all of this was to happen after eight years of law school. I was destined to become the best lawyer that money could buy. I had my entire life planned out and did not foresee anything getting in the way of my plans.

As I entered high school, those dreams seemed to fade fast and pretty soon were forgotten. I became lost in the shuffle of wanting to be popular, but at the same time not wanting to be seen. Sound confusing? It was. Imagine how it must have felt to a teenager, like others my age, who had no idea who they were. I wanted to be popular for social reasons. I figured if I was, I would always have friends. But, because I knew I was different (always have been), I wanted to hide in the corner so no one would notice me. I really can't explain how I was different; I just always felt I was. I never fit in and when I did, I was uncomfortable.

I was so engulfed in figuring out if I should fit in or not, that I began to wrestle with who I was and questioned where I belonged, in a sense. But, that was only half the struggle and the least of my problems. The main issue that caused me to lose sight of my dreams came way before high school. At the age of eight, my life significantly changed when my parents got divorced. The only two people I depended on were going their separate ways. My trust in depending on my Mom and Dad as a team to care for me, had been disturbed. My security blanket of parental togetherness had been snatched from under me. I was no longer dreaming about my future because there was something missing in my present. The attention, validation and love I needed as a young girl had, without warning, ceased and I was left searching for the one thing I was missing, love.

I spent my adolescent years looking for someone to give me the time and love I yearned for. Trying to find someone to fill the emptiness became an everyday search. My heart told me if I found someone to love me, I wouldn't be so lonely. I was convinced my happiness could only be found in a guy and that it would take forever to find him. Then one day, there he was, "my happiness" sitting at the mall waiting for the bus. It did not take long for us to start a relationship and, of course, have sex.

The morning I found out I was pregnant still plays in my mind like an old fashioned film. I can see the black and white scenes and I hear the reel slowly turning, as if it were my heartbeat. I was in my junior year of high school, seventeen and clueless. I chased my best friend down after first period and whispered in her ear, "I'm pregnant!" She chuckled as she thought I was fooling her. I didn't try to convince her that I was telling the truth; I was certain the upcoming months, and my growing belly would.

Months after becoming pregnant, I dropped out of school. Not because I was concerned with other people's reactions but because I didn't think school was important. I felt I had everything I needed. A boyfriend who worshiped the ground I walked on and a baby developing inside of me who could give me the love I had been longing for. I was satisfied. "Finally I am receiving the love I have been searching for," I thought. Life was certain to change for the better now that I had everything I ever wanted. I was satisfied. Well, at least I was for a little while. With each pound gained, the satisfactory feeling of my new life began to diminish. I was left, once again, to search for what was missing.

As I witnessed my peers graduating without me, I thought of all the opportunities I was going to miss. Dreams of becoming a lawyer immediately came to remembrance and seemed out of reach simultaneously. But then I heard a calm voice whisper something quite life-changing in my ear, "Why are you limiting yourself just because you are pregnant?" That very second, I made up in my mind that my life was not over. No matter how challenging it would be, I decided I would be a good mother and I would succeed in life.

With my newfound motivation, my mindset quickly changed from thoughts of "I don't know if I can make it" to "I know I will make it!" I started to believe in myself and encouraged myself daily. I surrounded myself around people who believed in me, as well. People who would push me when I would question if I was strong enough to continue. But most importantly, I went back to my roots and began to pray. Prayer gave me confidence in who I was and what I could do. Prayer also comforted me and instilled in my spirit the assurance that I was not alone.

At the age of 19, I was the mother to a one year old son, on my second relationship, and now mother to a newborn baby girl. I was determined I would not be a statistic. Society assumed because I was a teen mother of two children, and not married, that I was incapable of being an exceptional parent. I went back to school and fought to finish. I worked full-time while living in the "projects." I worked hard to save so I could move my children into a nice home. I did all that, and more, while holding my son's hand and carrying my daughter on my hip. I was not going to let myself down and I surely wasn't going to let my children down. I had a responsibility and that was to excel. Despite my circumstances, negativity and non-supporting people, I was going to succeed.

It was a long journey with plenty of hurdles embellishing the way. Some hurdles I cleared with no problem, but some hurdles I broke and left lying in pieces. I realized that making mistakes along the way wasn't an issue, it was not learning from them that was. I was willing to learn and I would try over and over again until I got it right. What was important was not giving up. I learned from my mistakes and kept going. I was determined to grow and become the best mother I could be, despite statistics and those waiting for me to fail.

Dear Teen Mom,

Don't let anyone tell you that your life will never be the same. Don't allow the whispers and finger-pointing deter you from living a life of happiness and victory. Yes, there will be some challenges but you can conquer every last one! Will there be days where you feel like crying? Yes! Does being a teen mom require hard work? Yes! But, being a mom period requires the same! Will it require dedication? Yes! But, everything you need is already planted inside of you! You have all you need inside you to excel in motherhood. Reach deep inside and pull out the strength, courage and determination you already possess and apply them to everyday life. Strength to continue, courage to walk with your head held high and determination to become better than you were yesterday. If you haven't, finish school and graduate. Education is important and will help you to teach your child the importance of receiving an education, expand your opportunities and help you to secure a great job to provide for your child. Don't be afraid to ask for help from those who are supporting you. It really is fine! Asking for help does not mean you're a failure, it means you are smart enough to know when you need direction and guidance. That makes for a great parent! You have the same responsibility I did; to succeed. Do not let your age suggest that you are irresponsible. You are an exceptional parent, or will be one. Teen pregnancy is not the end of the world. Decide today that you will not limit yourself. Set an example for your precious child, because they will be watching. Don't put yourself down, instead be proud because we have turned something society deems tragic into something beautiful!

I have faith in you.
YOU will succeed.
YOU WILL succeed.
YOU WILL SUCCEED!
And....You will look cute doing it!

~ Lakeisha Bowling

MEET OUR AUTHORS

ALEXIS BATES

Alexis Bates is a mother to one beautiful girl. Alexis has been an honor student all her life and has been in the newspaper several times for her wonderful achievements. She has earned over $300,000 in scholarships after graduating high school with over 4.0 GPA. Alexis is now a full time college student, where she is studying Educational Studies with an emphasis in Early Childhood. She finds herself spending most of her time trying to make a change and thinking of a way to create a better future for herself and her daughter. She enjoys laughing, spending time with her friends and family and writing. This is her first time writing a book, but is honored to be able to share her journey. Alexis hopes to inspire all youth to find their path, never give up and to know that they are never alone.

LAKEISHA BOWLING

LaKeisha Bowling is an Advocate, Author and Motivational Speaker. She is the founder of "I Bleed Purple". An organization built to empower victims of domestic abuse to break the chains that bind their souls, minds and personal lives through activating truth found in the Word of God.

As a survivor of Domestic Abuse, LaKeisha utilizes her gifts as a motivational speaker in the fight against this horrible epidemic. Her speaking engagements are rooted in her very own personal experiences.

LaKeisha has been a guest on Erica Campbell's "GetupMorningswithErica" Radio Show, The Micheal Basiden Show, has been featured in various Magazine Features, Blog posts and Podcasts. LaKeisha recently filmed her life story with CBN for "The 700 Club" and appeared on Dr. Jamal Bryant's Show "Power 2 The People", broadcasted on The Word Network. For booking information, please email Hepaidnfull@gmail.com. Visit my Website at www.freeandfearless.net.

SANA COTTEN

Sana Latrease is an overcomer of molestation and a product of the foster care system, Sana Latrease stands boldly in her truth. She is considered to be the Harriet Tubman of her generation because she has accepted the call to lead women of all generations, out of bondage, to Freedom in Christ Jesus. Sana's mission is to divinely connect, inspire, and empower women through all walks of life to be their healed and whole selves. She is the Founder of Pearls of Grace, a foundation that empowers women to Freedom and Purpose in Christ. She is also an Advocate for Adopted and foster children as well as Children of Incarcerated Parents. Alongside her husband, Sana serves as the Assistant Director of Camp Shiloh, an affordable, state licensed, youth summer camp and Shiloh Youth Enrichment Program, a before and After School Program that focuses on enriching the lives of the youth through homework assistance, and mentorship. Sana Latrease is the wife to Joshua E. Cotten and the mother of two beautiful children, Jamir and Janai. Sana's dedication to the power of God is most evident in her own testimony.

WHIT DEVERAUX

Whit Devereaux is an author, blogger, domestic violence survivor, and empowerment speaker. As the mother of two, she enjoys taking family vacations and spending quality time with her daughters. She is an advocate for families of children with special needs and works with underserved individuals to get access to quality health care. Her desire is to inspire, educate and empower those who are in abusive relationships to be free and enter into a personal relationship with our Father in Heaven. Whit Devereaux tells her journey in overcoming abuse and becoming one with God through her blogs. As a woman who once struggled with low self-esteem, teenage pregnancy, and abuse at the hands of those who claimed to love her, she knows first-hand what it takes to overcome it all. God still has a purpose beyond the pain and can use even you to show someone else that it can be done. For booking information email info@whitdeveraux.com or via the contact form on www.whitdevereaux.com.

YERINITA CURTIS-FULLER

Yerinita Curtis Fuller is a gifted writer and teacher. Possessing a true aptness to encourage, empower, and uplift, she has mentored others for over a decade. She has an AA Degree in Human Services Management, is currently pursuing a degree in Psychology and works for the Chicago Public School system. Yerinita and her husband, Larry, reside in the Chicagoland area where they raise their seven beautiful children.

AVERY RAYNOR

Avery is an author and mother of three beautiful children. She loves to encourage other young mothers with her wisdom and life experiences. She is blessed to give her children the best life possible.

CHRSTINA WORTH

Christina L. Worth is a mother, an inspirational speaker, an author and a mentor. She is vibrant, radical, and passionate about empowering young ladies. Through her gifts, God birthed Mahogany Angels a Non-Profit organization which Christina serves as the Founder and a mentor. She strives to encourage, empower, and equip young ladies between the ages of 8-17 years of age from all walks of life to be their best self. Christina has had her share of struggles in life, but is continuously evolving, and is experiencing the victories that come from the renewal of the mind, body and soul only through God's love. Through her TRUTH her aspirations are to encourage someone to discover their purpose, passion, and inner strength. When Christina is not changing lives, she enjoys singing, relaxing, and spending quality time with friends and family. For booking information email Christina.Worth@yahoo.com.

There's A Jewel In You, Volume 3

This is an amazing opportunity to become a published author or add another book to your resume. This movement is changing the lives of young mothers across the world. This project is no walk in the park. You will have to manage your time wisely and participate in the group discussions. **Submission for TAJIY Volume 3 will open up in late 2018.**

Here are the 2019 application requirements of the anthology:

1. $75 registration fee (non-refundable) due upon acceptance.
2. A professional headshot in PNG format. (NO EXCEPTIONS)
3. Website (NO EXCEPTIONS)

CHANTEA WILLIAMS

Chantea M. Williams is a chef, author, publisher, speaker and mentor, who loves encouraging women and teen mothers to become greater through the word of God. Through her gifts God created the Greater Working Women Ministries. They strive to encourage, empower and equip women from all walks of life to live out their God given purpose with holy boldness. She does 8 minute devotions at 8 AM/EST Monday thru Friday on Periscope and Facebook to jumpstart your morning with a powerful word. Sign up for the bi-weekly newsletter at www.greaterwomen.com for upcoming events. For booking information email booking@greaterwomen.com.

Connect with Greater Working Women Ministries:

www.greaterwomen.com

info@greaterwomen.com

Follow us @greaterwomen on all social media

Get Your Write On

Have you always wanted to publish a book or coordinate an anthology but thought you had to have thousands to do so? We are here to assist you, so that you can get your message out to the world.

Schedule your complimentary book consultation today with Greater Working Women Publishing Company, LLC (GWWP) at www.gwwpublishing.com. You can also register for our Get Your Write On Course, where you will be able to publish an e-book on Kindle upon completion.

We partner with Christian and inspirational authors to turn their dreams of publishing a reality. For more information on our publishing package please email us at info@gwwpublishing.com.

~We take care of the publishing while you take care of the public appearances.~

www.ingramcontent.com/pod-product-compliance
Lightning Source LLC
LaVergne TN
LVHW051848080426
835512LV00018B/3140